bake me I'm yours…
push pop
cakes

Katie Deacon

David and Charles

www.stitchcraftcreate.co.uk

contents

introduction...

Cupcakes are a phenomenon – they have been taking the world by storm and nothing seems to stand in their way. Cupcakes not only look and taste delicious but they're making way for some new and exciting ideas. First came cake pops, now welcome their super cute big sister the cupcake push pop! As soon as I discovered the premise of combining my passion for baking with my nostalgic, child-of-the-90s memories, I was hooked. Layers of cake sandwiched together with frosting, just like a regular cupcake but in a no-fuss container, what's not to love?

Push pops undeniably look impressive but they're practical too. Easy to transport and store, they're perfect for kids of all ages and make the ideal gift for a special occasion. Within this book I've included decorations and flavours that can be used for a whole host of events and celebrations, from Christmas to weddings. My aim is for these designs to provide you with a creative platform and inspire you to devise your own push pop masterpieces.

I really hope you have as much fun with these adorable little treats as I did thinking them up. Each project has a difficulty rating indicated by one, two or three spoons so that bakers of all levels of experience can dive in head first.

Keep sweet.

Katie xo

tools & equipment

Before you start, it's probably a good idea to look through the book and make a note of any equipment you have and what you need. Here is a basic list that will help you create all of the projects featured.

♡ Electric hand whisk or freestanding mixer – for mixing cake batters

♡ Mini cupcake tin (pan) – all of the recipes make 24 mini cupcakes, so either choose a 24-cup one or buy two 12-cup tins to save you baking time

♡ Teaspoons – perfect size for measuring out your batter

♡ Wire rack – to cool cupcakes

♡ Food colour – paste is always best, as it won't affect the consistency of cake batters and frostings

- Cocktail sticks (toothpicks) – for adding food colour and indenting paste decorations
- Non-stick rolling pin – for rolling out your sugarpaste (rolled fondant) and flower (petal/gum) paste
- Craft knife – for cutting out paste shapes by hand
- Cutters and plunger cutters – it's a good idea to collect a few different designs
- Palette knife – For lifting and turning paste pieces

- Edible glue – for sticking paste shapes together
- Edible ink pens – for adding small detailing
- Small paintbrushes – for applying water, lustre dust and edible glue to paste decorations, and cornflour (cornstarch) to moulds
- Foam mat – for drying paste decorations
- Piping (pastry) bags – disposable is always best for ease of clean-up

- Piping tubes (tips) – for decorating; try to get a set with a few different sizes
- Push pop containers
- Perspex push pop stand – for decorating and displaying your push pops

US cup measurements
If you prefer to use cup measurements, please use the following conversions. (Note. 1 Australian tbsp = 20ml.)

liquid
1 tsp = 5ml
1 tbsp = 15ml
1½ cup = 120ml/4fl oz
1 cup = 240/8½fl oz

butter
1 tbsp = 15g/½oz
2 tbsp = 25g/1oz
½ cup/1 stick = 115g/4oz
1 cup/2 sticks = 225g/8oz

caster (superfine) sugar/brown sugar
½ cup = 100g/3½oz
1 cup = 200g/7oz

sifted icing (confectioners') sugar
1 cup = 100g/3½oz

flour
1 cup = 125g/4½oz

cream cheese
1 cup = 230g/8oz

peanut butter
1 cup = 260g/9¼oz

recipes

So now you have your baking kit ready, it's time to decide which delicious cake flavour you want for your push pops, whether it's a classic like chocolate or something a bit more daring such as red velvet. Then simply choose a luxurious frosting to complement it – on offer are some exciting variations on the beloved traditional butttercream, including peanut butter and rose-flavoured!

vanilla

These vanilla mini cupcakes will always deliver, but I've also suggested some twists on the traditional flavouring for when you fancy something just a bit different.

you will need...
makes 24 mini cupcakes

- 175g (6oz) self-raising (-rising) flour
- 25g (1oz) plain (all-purpose) flour
- 1 tsp baking powder
- 175g (6oz) unsalted butter, softened
- 175g (6oz) caster (superfine) sugar
- 3 large free-range eggs
- 1 tsp (5ml) vanilla extract
- 3 tbsp (45ml) milk

1 Preheat the oven to 180°C/fan 160°C/350°F/Gas Mark 4. Spray the cups of your mini cupcake tin(s) (pan(s)) with cake release spray or grease with butter.

2 Sift both flours and the baking powder together into a bowl.

3 In a separate bowl and using an electric hand whisk, or using a freestanding mixer, beat the butter and sugar together for about 5 minutes until light and fluffy.

4 Add the eggs one at a time, mixing thoroughly between each addition. If the batter begins to curdle, add 1 tablespoon of the flour mixture after each egg. Add the vanilla extract and mix well.

5 Add the flour mixture all at once and fold into the batter. Add the milk and mix to combine.

6 Using 2 teaspoons, fill each cupcake cup two-thirds full. Bake in the oven for 15 minutes, or until the cupcakes are risen, golden and firm to the touch. Allow to cool in the tin for 5 minutes, then use a small palate knife to remove the cupcakes and transfer to a wire rack to cool completely.

make it different
lemon: Add 2 tsp grated lemon zest with the vanilla extract.
amaretto: Replace the vanilla extract with 1 tsp (5ml) almond extract.

chocolate

There's nothing nicer than a choccy cupcake and this is such an easy, dependable recipe. Chocolate lovers are also sure to enjoy the variations on the basic flavour theme.

you will need...
makes 24 mini cupcakes

- ♡ 175g (6oz) self-raising (-rising) flour
- ♡ 50g (1¾oz) cocoa powder (unsweetened cocoa)
- ♡ 1 tsp baking powder
- ♡ 175g (6oz) unsalted butter, softened
- ♡ 100g (3½) caster (superfine) sugar
- ♡ 75g (2¾oz) light brown sugar
- ♡ 3 large free-range eggs
- ♡ 1 tsp (5ml) vanilla extract
- ♡ 3 tbsp (45ml) milk

1 Preheat the oven to 180°C/fan 160°C/350°F/Gas Mark 4. Spray the cups of your mini cupcake tin(s) (pan(s)) with cake release spray or grease with butter.

2 Sift the flour, cocoa and baking powder together into a bowl.

3 In a separate bowl and using an electric hand whisk, or using a freestanding mixer, beat the butter and both sugars together until light and fluffy.

4 Add the eggs one at a time, mixing thoroughly between each addition. If the batter begins to curdle, add 1 tablespoon of the flour mixture after each egg. Add the vanilla extract and mix well.

5 Add the flour mixture all at once and fold into the batter. Add the milk and mix to combine.

6 Using 2 teaspoons, fill each cupcake cup two-thirds full. Bake in the oven for 15 minutes, or until the cupcakes are risen, golden and firm to the touch. Allow to cool in the tin for 5 minutes, then use a small palate knife to remove the cupcakes and transfer to a wire rack to cool completely.

make it different
chocolate cola: Replace the milk with 3 tbsp (45ml) soda stream cola syrup.
chocolate orange: Add 1 tsp (5ml) orange extract or 1 tbsp grated orange zest.

carrot

It's no wonder that the moist and moreish carrot cake is a firm favourite and this mini cupcake version won't disappoint. Plus it's the perfect vehicle for cream cheese frosting!

you will need...
makes 24 mini cupcakes

- ♡ 225g (8oz) carrots, peeled and finely grated
- ♡ 130g (4½oz) plain (all-purpose) flour
- ♡ 1½ tsp bicarbonate of soda (baking soda)
- ♡ 1 tsp baking powder
- ♡ 1½ tsp ground cinnamon
- ♡ 2 large free-range eggs
- ♡ 150g (5½ oz) light brown sugar
- ♡ 125ml (4fl oz) sunflower oil
- ♡ 1 tsp (5ml) vanilla extract

1 Preheat the oven to 180°C/fan 160°C/350°F/Gas Mark 4. Spray the cups of your mini cupcake tin(s) (pan(s)) with cake release spray or grease with butter.

2 Wrap the grated carrot in a clean tea (dish) towel and squeeze out the excess water.

3 Sift the flour, bicarbonate of soda, baking powder and cinnamon together into a bowl.

4 In a separate bowl and using an electric hand whisk, or using a freestanding mixer, beat the eggs and sugar together. While still beating, gradually add the oil and vanilla extract.

5 Slowly add the flour mixture and continue to mix until incorporated. Add the grated carrot to the batter and stir in with a wooden spoon until evenly distributed.

6 Using 2 teaspoons, fill each cupcake cup two-thirds full. Bake in the oven for 15 minutes, or until the cupcakes are risen, golden and firm to the touch. Allow to cool in the tin for 5 minutes, then use a small palate knife to remove the cupcakes and transfer to a wire rack to cool completely.

red velvet

This is the recipe to go for when you really want to wow. The vibrant red sponge is creamy rich in buttermilk with just a hint of chocolate.

you will need...
makes 24 mini cupcakes

- 260g (9¼oz) plain (all-purpose) flour
- 2 tbsp cocoa powder (unsweetened cocoa)
- 1 tsp baking powder
- pinch of salt
- 250ml (9fl oz) buttermilk
- 1½ tsp red paste food colour
- 130g (4½ oz) unsalted butter, softened
- 250g (9oz) caster (superfine) sugar
- 2 large eggs
- 1 tsp bicarbonate of soda (baking soda)
- 1 tsp (5ml) white wine vinegar

1 Preheat the oven to 180°C/fan 160°C/350°F/Gas Mark 4. Spray the cups of your mini cupcake tin(s) (pan(s)) with cake release spray or grease with butter.

2 Sift the flour, cocoa, baking powder and salt together into a bowl. In a separate bowl, mix the buttermilk and red paste food colour together.

3 In another bowl and using an electric hand whisk, or using a freestanding mixer, beat the butter and sugar together until pale and creamy. With the speed on high, add the eggs and beat for a few minutes. Add half of the flour mixture, followed by all of the buttermilk mixture and then the remainder of the flour mixture. Mix well to combine.

4 Working quickly, in a small bowl, mix the bicarbonate of soda and vinegar together, allowing it to fizz up slightly before adding it to the cake batter. Quickly fold in.

5 Using 2 teaspoons, fill each cupcake cup two-thirds full. Bake in the oven for 15 minutes, or until the cupcakes are risen, golden and firm to the touch. Allow to cool in the tin for 5 minutes, then use a small palate knife to remove the cupcakes and transfer to a wire rack to cool completely.

banana

Here is the ideal opportunity to rescue those forgotten bananas from the fruit bowl and transform them into mouthwatering mini treats.

you will need...
makes 24 mini cupcakes

- ♡ 250g (9oz) plain (all-purpose) flour
- ♡ 2 tsp baking powder
- ♡ 125g (4½oz) unsalted butter, softened
- ♡ 250g (9oz) caster (superfine) sugar
- ♡ 2 large free-range eggs
- ♡ 1 tsp (5ml) vanilla extract
- ♡ 4 overripe bananas, mashed with a fork

1 Preheat the oven to 180°C/fan 160°C/350°F/Gas Mark 4. Spray the cups of your mini cupcake tin(s) (pan(s)) with cake release spray or grease with butter.

2 Sift the flour and baking powder together into a bowl.

3 In a separate bowl and using an electric hand whisk, or using a freestanding mixer, beat the butter and sugar together for about 5 minutes until light and fluffy.

4 Add the eggs one at a time, mixing thoroughly between each addition. If the batter begins to curdle, add 1 tablespoon of the flour mixture after each egg. Add the vanilla extract and mix well.

5 Add the flour mixture all at once and fold into the batter. Add the mashed banana and mix until evenly combined.

6 Using 2 teaspoons, fill each cupcake cup two-thirds full. Bake in the oven for 15 minutes, or until the cupcakes are risen, golden and firm to the touch. Allow to cool in the tin for 5 minutes, then use a small palate knife to remove the cupcakes and transfer to a wire rack to cool completely.

vanilla buttercream

Sometimes the best choice of frosting is the purity of taste that only vanilla buttercream can offer. But at other times you'll want a double hit of your chosen flavour, such as lemon mini cupcakes with zingy lemon buttercream.

you will need...

- ♡ 125g (4½oz) unsalted butter, softened
- ♡ 350g (12oz) icing (confectioners') sugar, sifted
- ♡ 1 tsp (5ml) vanilla extract
- ♡ 2–3 tbsp (30–45ml) milk

1 Beat the butter in a large bowl with an electric hand whisk, or using a freestanding mixer, until light and fluffy.

2 While still beating, add the sugar a tablespoon at a time, followed by the vanilla extract and milk, until you have the desired consistency.

make it different

mint: Replace vanilla with 1 tsp (5ml) peppermint extract. Tint the frosting mint green using a cocktail stick (toothpick) dipped into green paste food colour.

lemon: Add 2 tsp finely grated lemon zest, and 1 tbsp (15ml) lemon juice if you like it really citrusy, to the frosting – reduce the milk by 1 tbsp (15ml) if adding the lemon juice.

amaretto: Replace the vanilla extract with 1 tsp (5ml) almond extract.

rose: Replace the vanilla extract with 1 tsp (5ml) rose extract.

chocolate buttercream

It really is worth purchasing a good-quality dark cocoa powder for this frosting to ensure an ultra-rich chocolatey flavour.

you will need...

- ♥ 125g (4½oz) unsalted butter, softened
- ♥ 300g (10½oz) icing (confectioners') sugar, sifted
- ♥ 50g (1¾oz) cocoa powder (unsweetened cocoa), sifted
- ♥ 1 tsp (5ml) vanilla extract
- ♥ 2–3 tbsp (30–45ml) milk

1 Beat the butter in a large bowl with an electric hand whisk, or using a freestanding mixer, until light and fluffy.

2 While still beating, add the sugar and cocoa a tablespoon at a time, followed by the vanilla and milk, until you have the desired consistency.

make it different
chocolate orange: Add 1 tsp (5ml) orange extract or 1 tbsp grated orange zest.

cookies & cream buttercream

This is a ridiculously decadent yet easy frosting option for all those who just can't get enough of their favourite chocolate sandwich cookie.

you will need...

- ♡ 125g (4½oz) unsalted butter, softened
- ♡ 350g (12oz) icing (confectioners') sugar, sifted
- ♡ 1 tsp (5ml) vanilla extract
- ♡ 2–3 tbsp (30–45ml) milk
- ♡ 7 Oreo cookies, crushed to crumbs in a food processor or with a rolling pin in a plastic bag

1 Beat the butter in a large bowl with an electric hand whisk, or using a freestanding mixer, until light and fluffy.

2 While still beating, add the sugar a tablespoon at a time, followed by the vanilla extract and milk, until you have the desired consistency. Add the Oreo cookie crumbs and mix until combined.

cream cheese frosting

This super-creamy frosting is the perfect match for your carrot mini cupcakes but would work equally well with the red velvet or chocolate ones.

you will need...

- ♡ 125g (4½oz) unsalted butter, softened
- ♡ 200g (7oz) cream cheese
- ♡ 500g (1lb 2oz) icing (confectioners') sugar, sifted
- ♡ 1 tsp (5ml) vanilla extract

1 Beat the butter and cream cheese together in a large bowl with an electric hand whisk, or using a freestanding mixer, until combined.

2 While still beating, add the sugar a tablespoon at a time, followed by the vanilla extract, until you have the desired consistency. Take care not to over-beat, as cream cheese frosting has a tendency to become runny.

make it different
cinnamon cream cheese: Add 1 tsp ground cinnamon at the same time as the vanilla extract.

peanut butter buttercream

Frosting doesn't come much more indulgent than this. It makes an especially good pairing with the chocolate mini cupcakes both in flavour and appearance.

you will need...

- 💙 125g (4½oz) unsalted butter, softened
- 💙 150g (5½oz) smooth peanut butter
- 💙 350g (12oz) icing (confectioners') sugar, sifted
- 💙 1 tsp (5ml) vanilla extract
- 💙 2–3 tbsp (30–45ml) milk

1 Beat the butter and peanut butter together in a large bowl with an electric hand whisk, or using a freestanding mixer, until light and fluffy.

2 While still beating, add the sugar a tablespoon at a time, followed by the vanilla extract and milk, until you have the desired consistency.

swiss meringue buttercream

This is a bit more involved to make than ordinary buttercream, but the extra effort will be rewarded by a silky smooth, light and seductive frosting.

you will need...

- ♡ 170g (6oz) caster (superfine) sugar
- ♡ 3 egg whites
- ♡ ⅛ tsp salt
- ♡ 170g (6oz) unsalted butter, at room temperature

make it different
coffee: Dissolve 2 tsp instant espresso in 1 tbsp (15ml) boiling water. Allow to cool to room temperature and add at the end. Mix for 1 minute to reduce air bubbles.

1 Place the sugar, egg whites and salt in the top of a double boiler over a pan of simmering water. Whisking continuously, cook until the sugar has dissolved and the mixture is warm (about 160°C/325°F).

2 Using a freestanding mixer fitted with the whisk attachment, beat the egg white mixture on high speed until it forms stiff (but not dry) peaks. Continue beating until fluffy and cooled – about 7 minutes in total.

3 Switch to the paddle attachment. With the mixer on medium-low speed, add the butter 25g (1oz) at a time, beating well after each addition. Increase the speed to medium-high and continue beating the frosting for about 3 minutes until it looks thick.

techniques

Once you have baked your mini cupcakes and prepared your frosting, the next stage is the thrilling creative one. Here I first show you how to fill and frost your cakes in order to assemble your push pops, and then take you through the various ways in which you can decorate them. These include using cutters and moulds, simple piping, and embellishing with edible glitter and lustre dust.

making push pops

Follow these simple steps to make your basic push pops ready for adding any kind of decoration you choose.

1 Ensure your cupcakes are all roughly the same size. Trim any pieces where the cupcake has risen above the cupcake tin (pan).

2 Fit your piping (pastry) bag with your chosen piping tube (tip) (most of the projects use a no. 1m (WIL) or a plain round 1cm (½in) tube) and fill with buttercream.

3 Place one cupcake in the bottom of your push pop container and pipe a layer of frosting on top, starting in the centre of the cupcake working round in a small circle before releasing pressure

and pulling up to stop the flow. Top with another cupcake and repeat the frosting step but continue piping upwards in decreasing circles.

4 If instructed in the projects to pipe your cupcakes high, use a round 1cm (½in) piping tube and create a tall mound of frosting about 3cm (1¼in) high for your sugarpaste (rolled fondant) lid to sit on comfortably.

5 Place your push pop in a Perspex push pop stand to decorate and display. If you don't have one, a Champagne flute is the perfect substitute.

colouring

Even before you begin decorating, you can bring drama to your push pops by splitting your cake batter and colouring it varying shades. Then you can move on to experimenting with tinting your frosting to mix or match.

Colouring cake batters

When colouring cake batters, always use paste food colour rather than liquid, as this can affect the consistency of your mixture. Add the colour using a cocktail stick (toothpick), a tiny amount at a time – it's easier to add colour than to take it away.

You can colour the cakes for your push pops in two different ways. The first is to split the prepared mixture for 24 mini cupcakes into separate bowls, colouring each bowl to your desired shade and then baking as instructed. Alternatively, you can divide the batter between two or three sandwich (round shallow) cake tins (pans) about 23cm (9in) in diameter lined with baking (parchment) paper and dye each to the desired colour. Bake in an oven preheated to 160°C/fan 140°C/325°F/Gas Mark 3 for 20 minutes. Once cool, trim the domed tops off your cakes and cut out rounds with an empty push pop container before assembling.

Colouring frostings

Paste food colour is also ideal for colouring buttercream and royal icing, and again it's important to add it in tiny amounts in the same way until you achieve the shade you want.

decorating

The various designs featured in this book have all been created using just a few basic decorating techniques, and if you haven't yet done so, it won't take you long to master them. You can then use these skills to develop your own decorative schemes.

Rolling out paste

Rolling out your sugarpaste (rolled fondant) or flower (petal/gum) paste can be done in one of two ways. The first method is to lightly dust your work surface with icing (confectioners') sugar before taking your pliable paste, placing it on the dusted surface and rolling it out with a non-stick rolling pin. If using this method, remember to turn your paste after each roll of your rolling pin to prevent it from sticking.

Method number two is the lazy guy's guide to rolling paste – it's easier to clean up and requires no special equipment. Just take two sheets of cling film (plastic wrap), place your paste between the sheets and roll out using a rolling pin. Pull the cling film flat after each roll to prevent the paste bursting out of the sides.

Using cutters

When using cutters, roll out your flower (petal/gum) paste or sugarpaste (rolled fondant) to the thickness specified and then place the cutter on top. Press down firmly and give the cutter a little wiggle to make sure you get a sharp edge. If you have a more complex cutter shape, you can lay the paste over the cutting edge of your cutter and roll a rolling pin over the shape to create a clean edge. To remove the shape, give it a little nudge with the end of a paintbrush.

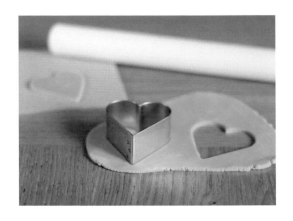

Plunger cutters are just like other cutters but with the added bonus of imprinting your finished shape with indentations and veins. Use just like a normal cutter, but once you have cut your shape out, press down firmly on the plunger before pulling up and ejecting the shape by pumping the button. Leave to dry on a foam mat, or on a folded piece of card if your paste pieces need shaping.

Cutting paste by hand

When cutting out paste shapes by hand, always remember to use a very sharp craft knife, otherwise you risk wrinkling your paste. Try to avoid hand-cutting paste on very humid days, as the paste will soon become very sticky and hard to work with. If this happens, place the rolled-out paste in the fridge for 30 minutes before attempting to cut again.

Shaping flowers

The best way to shape a flower is to invest in a plastic paint palette, which has a series of round wells that are perfect for cupping your flowers while they dry. Simply cut out the flowers using your chosen cutter, then place each individual flower in a well of the palette to dry for several hours or overnight.

To shape smaller flowers, push a ball tool into the centre of each flower before leaving them to dry on a foam mat.

Using moulds

One of the easiest ways to create complex detailing for paste decorations is to use a mould. You can purchase moulds in a whole variety of different designs and themes to decorate your push pops, and they are super-easy to use.

First, use a small paintbrush to dust the cavity of the mould with cornflour (cornstarch) – this is to prevent the sugarpaste (rolled fondant) from sticking to the design. Knead a ball of sugarpaste until smooth and pliable, then press it into the mould. Trim off any excess paste with a sharp knife before tipping the mould upside down and letting the moulded shape fall out. Dust off any excess cornflour from the moulded shape with the paintbrush and leave your decoration to dry for several hours or overnight.

Moulded sugarpaste shapes can then be painted or decorated with edible lustre dusts or glitter.

Piping details

Piping is ideal for personalising your designs with initials or numbers, or for adding simple details to paste decorations.

Start by trimming the end off a disposable piping (pastry) bag and inserting a no. 2 piping tube (tip). Fill the bag with royal icing, either plain white or tinted with the appropriate paste food colour. Squeeze any remaining air from the bag and twist the end of the bag to tighten. Holding the bag like a pen, squeeze gently with constant pressure, ensuring that you hold the tube about 2.5cm (1in) above the surface you wish to decorate. The aim is to lay the icing on the surface rather than trying to write with it. Allow the piping to dry for about an hour.

Using wires

One thing to remember when using wires is that they should never be inserted directly into a cake and should always be removed before eating. To ensure that your wires are safely placed in your cake, use a small plastic cone called a posy pick. Simply push a small piece of flower (petal/gum) paste or sugarpaste (rolled fondant) into the tip of the posy pick before inserting the end of your wire to hold it steady. Remove the picks and wires before eating the cakes.

Glitter & dust

Edible glitter can add a touch of glitz and glamour to your projects, while lustre dust can be applied with a small paintbrush to paste shapes made using a cutter or mould to create subtle colouring effects. However, official food safety classifications in relation to glitter and lustre dust have recently changed and you should check these products to see whether they have been deemed 'edible', 'food-contact' or 'non-toxic', and follow the manufacturer's instructions for using accordingly.

fabulous flavours

mint chocolate chip

This classic flavour combination is sure to excite adults and children alike.

you will need...
makes 12

- ♡ **24 chocolate mini cupcakes**
- ♡ **1 batch mint buttercream tinted bright green with paste food colour**
- ♡ **100g (3½oz) plain (semisweet or bittersweet) chocolate chips**
- ♡ **4 mint-flavoured chocolate sticks**
- ♡ **disposable plastic piping (pastry) bag fitted with a no. 1M (WIL) piping tube (tip)**

1 Assemble each of your push pops, starting with a chocolate mini cupcake. Then place the green-tinted mint buttercream in the piping bag and pipe a swirl on top.

2 Sprinkle the buttercream swirl with a few chocolate chips, then top with another chocolate mini cupcake and pipe on more of the buttercream in a tall swirl.

3 Break each mint chocolate stick into thirds and insert two pieces into the top of each push pop.

Recipes mini cupcakes, frostings & fillings
Techniques making push pops, colouring frostings

mocha dream

Who needs a cup of coffee when you have these delightful push pops to perk you up in the morning.

you will need...

makes 12

- ♡ **24 chocolate mini cupcakes**
- ♡ **1 batch coffee Swiss meringue buttercream**
- ♡ **50g (1¾oz) cocoa powder (unsweetened cocoa)**
- ♡ **24 chocolate-covered coffee beans**
- ♡ **disposable plastic piping (pastry) bag fitted with a no. 1M (WIL) piping tube (tip)**

1 Assemble each of your push pops, starting with a chocolate mini cupcake. Then place the coffee Swiss meringue buttercream in the piping bag and pipe a swirl on top.

2 Repeat Step 1 but pipe on more buttercream in a tall swirl.

3 Decorate the top of each push pop with a dusting of cocoa and two chocolate-covered coffee beans.

Recipes mini cupcakes, frostings & fillings
Techniques making push pops

strawberries & cream

These gorgeous fresh strawberry push pops are perfect for a sunny afternoon garden party.

you will need...

makes 12

- ♡ 24 vanilla mini cupcakes
- ♡ strawberry jam in squeezy bottle
- ♡ 1 batch vanilla buttercream
- ♡ 12 large fresh strawberries
- ♡ disposable plastic piping (pastry) bag fitted with a 1cm (½in) round piping tube (tip)

1 Assemble each of your push pops, starting with a mini vanilla cupcake and adding a squirt of strawberry jam. Then place the vanilla buttercream in the piping bag and pipe a swirl on top.

2 Repeat Step 1 but pipe on more buttercream in a tall swirl.

3 Decorate the top of each push pop with a juicy strawberry.

seasonal sensations...
Change the fruits and jams according to what's in season or a good buy – blueberries, raspberries and blackberries would all work perfectly.

Recipes mini cupcakes, frostings & fillings
Techniques making push pops

eastern delight

The chocolate and rose complement each other beautifully in these exotic and romantic push pops.

you will need...

makes 12

- ♡ **24 chocolate mini cupcakes**
- ♡ **1 batch rose buttercream tinted pink with paste food colour**
- ♡ **1 bar Turkish Delight**
- ♡ **disposable plastic piping (pastry) bag fitted with a no. 1M (WIL) piping tube (tip)**

1 Assemble each of your push pops, starting with a chocolate mini cupcake. Then place the pink-tinted rose buttercream in the piping bag and pipe a swirl on top.

2 Repeat Step 1 but pipe on more buttercream in a tall swirl.

3 Cut 12 slivers from your Turkish Delight bar and then cut each sliver in half on the diagonal. Decorate the top of each push pop with two halves of the Turkish Delight, propping them up against each other.

Recipes mini cupcakes, frostings & fillings
Techniques making push pops, colouring frostings

cherry cola

Everyone enjoys a deep glug of cherry cola on a warm day, so why not mix it up a little and offer out these push pops instead.

you will need...

makes 12

- ♡ 24 mini chocolate cola cupcakes
- ♡ 1 batch vanilla buttercream
- ♡ 1 jar red and green cocktail cherries
- ♡ 1–2 tbsp icing (confectioners') sugar, if needed
- ♡ disposable plastic piping (pastry) bag fitted with a 1cm (½in) round piping tube (tip)

1 First, add 2 tablespoons of the syrup from your jar of cocktail cherries to the buttercream and mix to combine. If it turns the buttercream a little loose, add the icing (confectioners') sugar to stiffen it again. Place the buttercream in the piping bag.

2 Assemble each of your push pops, starting with a mini chocolate cola cupcake. Then pipe a swirl of the buttercream on top.

3 Repeat Step 2 but pipe on more buttercream in a tall swirl.

4 Decorate the top of each push pop with the red and green cocktail cherries from the jar, drained of syrup.

Recipes mini cupcakes, frostings & fillings
Techniques making push pops

cookies & cream

There's nothing better than a chocolate cookie dipped into an ice-cold glass of milk, and these push pops are the cake embodiment of such pleasure.

you will need...

makes 12

- ♡ 24 mini chocolate cupcakes
- ♡ 1 batch cookies & cream buttercream
- ♡ 12 mini Oreo cookies or chocolate cookies of your choice
- ♡ disposable plastic piping (pastry) bag fitted with a no. 1M (WIL) piping tube (tip)

1 Assemble each of your push pops, starting with a mini chocolate cupcake. Then pipe a swirl of the buttercream on top.

2 Repeat Step 1 but pipe on more of the buttercream in a tall swirl.

3 Decorate the top of each push pop with a mini Oreo or chocolate cookie of your choice so that it stands upright in the frosting.

Recipes mini cupcakes, frostings & fillings
Techniques making push pops

lemon & blueberry

This is a lovely fresh and fruity flavour combination that is sure to be a hit with everyone, and it looks so inviting too.

you will need...

makes 12

- ♡ **24 mini lemon cupcakes**
- ♡ **200g (7oz) fresh blueberries**
- ♡ **1 batch vanilla buttercream**
- ♡ **disposable plastic piping (pastry) bag fitted with a 1cm (½in) round piping tube (tip)**

1 First, mash 150g (5½oz) of the blueberries to a pulp in a bowl with a fork. Cover and place in the fridge for a minimum of 2 hours or overnight until jellified.

2 Add your chilled mashed blueberries to the vanilla buttercream and mix to combine.

3 Assemble each of your push pops, starting with a mini lemon cupcake. Then place the blueberry buttercream in the piping bag and pipe a swirl on top.

4 Repeat Step 3 but pipe on more buttercream in a tall swirl.

5 Decorate the push pops with the remaining whole blueberries.

Recipes mini cupcakes, frostings & fillings
Techniques making push pops

rainbow bright

These spectacular rainbow-coloured push pops are sure to brighten even the dullest of days.

you will need...

makes 12

- ♡ **24 mini vanilla cupcakes,** 6 coloured red, 6 coloured yellow, 6 coloured blue and 6 coloured green
- ♡ **1 batch vanilla buttercream**
- ♡ **rainbow sprinkles (nonpareils)**
- ♡ **disposable plastic piping (pastry) bag fitted with a no. 1M (WIL) piping tube (tip)**

1 First, slice each of your coloured cupcakes horizontally in half.

2 Assemble each of your push pops, starting with a red cupcake half. Then place the vanilla buttercream in the piping bag and pipe a swirl on top.

3 Repeat Step 2 with a yellow cupcake half, then a blue cupcake half and finally a green cupcake half, ending with a generous swirl of buttercream on top.

4 Decorate the push pops with rainbow sprinkles.

Recipes mini cupcakes, frostings & fillings
Techniques making push pops, colouring cake batters

popping occasions

pocketful of posies

Forget the predictable bunch of fresh flowers this Mother's Day and present your mum with a beautiful bouquet of edible petunias instead.

you will need...

makes 3

- ♡ 3 lemon filled and piped push pops
- ♡ 100g (3½oz) pale blue flower (petal/gum) paste
- ♡ *medium blue edible lustre dust
- ♡ petunia cutter and veiner
- ♡ paint palette

*If product not certified edible, please remove before eating

1 Roll out the pale blue flower paste very thinly and use a petunia cutter to cut out nine flowers. Place each flower into the veiner and close gently to indent and shape your petunia flower. Place each flower in the well of a paint palette and leave to dry for several hours or overnight.

2 Once dry, use a small paintbrush to paint the edible lustre dust onto each flower, starting in the centre of the flower and spreading out over the petals so that the colour becomes lighter as it reaches the edges.

3 Attach three petunia flowers to the top of each decorated push pop.

Recipes mini cupcakes, frostings & fillings
Techniques making push pops, rolling out paste, using cutters, shaping flowers, glitter & dust

suited up

Your dad is sure to appreciate these adorable sugar ties much more than his silk version this Father's Day.

you will need...

makes 1

- ♡ 1 vanilla push pop filled and piped with chocolate buttercream
- ♡ sugarpaste (rolled fondant): 25g (1oz) white, 35g (1¼oz) red
- ♡ 20g (¾oz) white royal icing
- ♡ disposable plastic piping (pastry) bag fitted with a no. 2 piping tube (tip)

1 To make the collar, roll out the white sugarpaste to around 6mm (¼in) thick. Cut out a long strip, then cut the ends diagonally away from each other. Form the collar into a circle and position on top of your filled and piped push pop.

2 For the tie, roll out the red sugarpaste to around 4mm (³⁄₁₆in) thick, slightly thinner than your collar. Using a very sharp craft knife, cut out a tie shape.

3 Place the royal icing in the piping bag and pipe diagonal stripes down the length of your tie. Leave to dry for several hours or overnight.

4 Position the tie just beneath the collar so that the tail of the tie hangs down the push pop container.

Recipes mini cupcakes, frostings & fillings

Techniques making push pops, rolling out paste, cutting paste by hand, colouring frostings, piping details

graduation day

Give your successful scholar an extra award by creating these appropriately formal-looking push pops.

you will need...

makes 1

- ♡ 1 filled and piped push pop of your choice
- ♡ 20g (¾oz) black sugarpaste (rolled fondant)
- ♡ small amount of royal icing tinted black with paste food colour
- ♡ disposable plastic piping (pastry) bags fitted with a no. 2 piping tube (tip)

1 Form half of the black sugarpaste into the base of the graduation cap, flattening off the top for the mortarboard.

2 Reserving a small piece, for the mortarboard, roll out the remaining black sugarpaste to around 5mm (³⁄₁₆in) thick and cut out a square large enough to fit on the base of your cap.

3 Roll the reserved sugarpaste into a tapered sausage. Using a craft knife, carefully shred the thicker end to create a tassel. Place the black-tinted royal icing in the piping bag and attach the tassel to the top of your mortarboard with a little of the icing. Leave to dry overnight.

4 Once dry, attach the mortarboard to the cap base with some more black-tinted royal icing.

5 Position the graduation cap on top of your filled and piped push pop.

Recipes mini cupcakes, frostings & fillings

Techniques making push pops, rolling out paste, cutting paste by hand, colouring frostings

birthday bows

All wrapped up with a pretty little bow, who wouldn't be delighted with these gorgeous edible gifts.

you will need...

makes 1

- ♡ 1 filled and piped push pop of your choice
- ♡ 40g (1½oz) pink sugarpaste (rolled fondant)

1 Roll out the pink sugarpaste to around 4mm (³/₁₆in) thick and cut out a strip measuring 2.5cm x 7cm (1in x 2¾in) and another measuring 5mm x 3cm (¼in x 1¼in).

2 Take the larger strip of sugarpaste and fold each end into the centre, then pinch gently to create the bow shape. Wrap the smaller strip of sugarpaste around the middle of your bow, securing on the back with a dab of water.

3 Roll out the remaining pink sugarpaste to the same thickness. Cut two more strips measuring 2cm x 5cm (¾in x 2in) to create the tails of your bow, cutting a small 'V' shape out of one end of each strip.

4 Attach the tails to the top of the filled and piped push pop, followed by the bow, pressing down gently to secure.

Recipes mini cupcakes, frostings & fillings
Techniques making push pops, rolling out paste, cutting paste by hand

up, up & away

This uplifting balloon embellishment is suitable for all sorts of occasions, from a special birthday to a bon voyage send-off.

you will need...

makes 1

- ♡ 1 filled and piped push pop of your choice
- ♡ flower (petal/gum) paste: 15g (½oz) each red, blue and yellow
- ♡ 3 lengths of florist wire, 4cm (1½in) each
- ♡ 3 posy picks
- ♡ *edible glitter: red, blue, gold
- ♡ white sprinkles (nonpareils)

*If product not certified edible, please remove before eating

1 Roll out each flower paste colour thinly. Cut out two balloon shapes from each colour.

2 Spread a little edible glue over one balloon of each colour and place a florist wire down the centre. Sandwich each wire with a matching-coloured balloon, pressing down gently to seal.

3 Moisten each balloon with a little water and sprinkle with the corresponding-coloured edible glitter. Leave the balloons to dry for several hours or overnight.

4 Dip the top of your filled and piped push pop into white sprinkles. Push a small piece of flower paste into the tip of each posy pick, then insert the posy picks into the top of your push pop. Insert the wire stems of the balloons into the posy picks. Remove the posy picks and balloons before eating the cakes.

Recipes mini cupcakes, frostings & fillings

Techniques making push pops, rolling out paste, cutting paste by hand, using wires, glitter & dust

you're how old?

This sparkling design is ideal for marking those milestone birthdays, or use it instead for celebrating an anniversary.

you will need...

makes 1

- ♡ 1 filled and piped push pop of your choice
- ♡ 15g (½oz) red flower (petal/gum) paste
- ♡ *red edible glitter
- ♡ 2 lengths of florist wire, 4cm (1⅛in) each
- ♡ number cutters
- ♡ 2 posy picks

*If product not certified edible, please remove before eating

1 Roll out the red flower paste very thinly. Using number cutters, cut out the number shapes you need to form the age or number of years you are celebrating, cutting two of each.

2 Spread a little edible glue over one of each number shape and place a florist wire down the centre. Sandwich each wire with the corresponding second number shape, pressing down gently to seal.

3 Moisten each number with a little water and sprinkle with red edible glitter. Leave to dry for several hours or overnight.

4 Push a small piece of flower paste into the tip of each posy pick, then insert the posy picks into the centre of your filled and piped push pop. Insert the wire stems of the numbers into the posy picks. Remove the posy picks and numbers before eating the cakes.

Recipes mini cupcakes, frostings & fillings

Techniques making push pops, rolling out paste, cutting paste by hand, using wires, glitter & dust

beautiful bouquet

Daisies are the essence of fresh, sunny springtime, so present a delightful bunch of these push pops to celebrate any special occasion at that time of year.

you will need...

makes 5

- ♡ 5 filled and piped push pops of your choice
- ♡ 50g (1¾oz) white flower (petal/gum) paste
- ♡ 15g (½oz) yellow sugarpaste (rolled fondant)
- ♡ large sunflower plunger cutter
- ♡ paint palette with at least 5 wells

1 Roll out the white flower paste very thinly. Using the plunger cutter, cut out 10 flowers.

2 Place five of the flowers into separate wells of the paint palette, moisten the centre of each flower and place another daisy slightly offset on top of the first so that all the petals are visible.

3 Roll five small balls of yellow sugarpaste, flatten each into a disc, then indent small holes with a cocktail stick (toothpick). Using a dab of water, attach a disc to the centre of each daisy. Leave to dry overnight.

4 Position a flower on each of your filled and piped push pops and arrange to form a beautiful bouquet.

Recipes mini cupcakes, frostings & fillings
Techniques making push pops, rolling out paste, using cutters

cameo chic

These elegant push pops are simply perfect for a sophisticated afternoon tea with the girls – pot of Earl Grey tea optional.

you will need...

makes 1

- ♡ 1 filled and piped push pop of your choice
- ♡ 50g (1¾oz) white sugarpaste (rolled fondant)
- ♡ cornflour (cornstarch), for dusting
- ♡ *edible lustre dusts: gold, dark apricot
- ♡ silicone cameo mould

*If product not certified edible, please remove before eating

1 Using a small paintbrush, brush the inside of your cameo mould with cornflour to prevent the sugarpaste from sticking to the design. Take the white sugarpaste and press it firmly into the mould.

2 Release the cameo by turning the mould upside down. Dust off any cornflour left on the cameo with the paintbrush.

3 Again using the paintbrush, paint the outside 'frame' of the cameo with gold edible lustre dust. Clean your paintbrush, then carefully paint the negative space around the lady with dark apricot edible lustre dust. Leave the cameo to dry for a few hours or overnight.

4 Position the cameo on top of your filled and piped push pop.

Recipes mini cupcakes, frostings & fillings
Techniques making push pops, using moulds, glitter & dust

love birds

These wonderfully romantic, symbolic push pops are perfect for any wedding celebration.

you will need...

makes 1

- 1 vanilla push pop filled and piped with amaretto buttercream tinted pale green with paste food colour
- 20g (¾oz) white sugarpaste (rolled fondant)
- large dove plunger cutter
- black edible ink pen
- folded piece of card
- pale green translucent narrow ribbon

1 Take one-third of the sugarpaste and form into a small oval. Place the oval in the body cavity of the dove plunger cutter. Roll out the remaining sugarpaste to 3mm (⅛in) thick and cut out the dove shape using the end of the plunger. Press the plunger down firmly to join the body to the wings and make the feather impressions.

2 Eject the dove from the cutter and sharpen the beak using your fingers. Add the eye and beak detail with a black edible ink pen. Leave the dove to dry overnight in a folded piece of card.

3 Gently position the dove on top of the filled and piped push pop.

4 Tie a length of pale green translucent ribbon in a bow around the tube part of the push pop container.

Recipes mini cupcakes, frostings & fillings
Techniques making push pops, colouring frostings, using cutters

sensational seasons

snowflake wishes

These stunning snowflakes perfectly evoke those magical snowy days where you have nothing better to do than curl up with a good book and a warming drink.

you will need...

makes 1

- ♡ 1 vanilla push pop filled and piped with mint buttercream tinted pale green with paste food colour
- ♡ sugarpaste (rolled fondant): 20g (¾oz) each white and aqua
- ♡ icing (confectioners') sugar, for dusting
- ♡ large and medium veined snowflake plunger cutter

1 Roll out each sugarpaste colour to 3mm (⅛in) thick. Using the large snowflake plunger cutter, cut out a white snowflake, then use the medium plunger cutter to cut out an aqua snowflake.

2 Apply a small dab of water to the centre of the white snowflake, then place the smaller aqua snowflake on top, slightly off centre. Leave to dry overnight on a board dusted with icing sugar.

3 Position the snowflake on top of your filled and piped push pop.

all that glistens...

For a subtle shimmering effect, paint the snowflakes with cooled boiled water and dust sparingly with iridescent white edible glitter. If the product used is not certified edible, please remove the snowflake before eating the cake.

Recipes mini cupcakes, frostings & fillings
Techniques making push pops, colouring frostings, using cutters, glitter & dust

christmas pudding

These festive push pops are ideal for little ones who don't like the taste of traditional Christmas or plum pudding.

you will need...

makes 1

- ♡ 1 chocolate filled and piped push pop
- ♡ sugarpaste (rolled fondant): 20g (¾oz) brown, 10g (¼oz) white, 5g (⅛oz) red, 7g (generous ⅛oz) green
- ♡ 7cm (2¾in) circle cutter
- ♡ medium holly leaf plunger cutter

1 Roll out the brown sugarpaste to 2mm (¹⁄₁₆in) thick. Use the circle cutter, to cut out a circle. Gently place the circle on the filled and piped push pop and smooth it down to create a mound.

2 Roll out the white sugarpaste as before. Using a very sharp craft knife, cut out a 'splat' shape measuring around 3cm (1¼in) in diameter. Attach to the centre of the brown sugarpaste-covered push pop with a dab of water.

3 For berries, roll the red sugarpaste into three balls and attach to the centre of the white sugarpaste with a dab of water.

4 Roll out the green sugarpaste as before. Using the plunger cutter, cut out two holly leaves. Attach the leaves to the top of the push pop next to the berries.

Recipes mini cupcakes, frostings & fillings

Techniques making push pops, rolling out paste, using cutters, cutting paste by hand

pumpkin patch

Pumpkins aren't just for Halloween. These realistic-looking ones would go down well at a harvest supper or Thanksgiving celebration.

you will need...

makes 1

- ♡ 1 filled and piped push pop of your choice
- ♡ sugarpaste (rolled fondant): 30g (generous 1oz) orange, 5g (⅛oz) brown

1 Roll the orange sugarpaste into a ball and flatten it slightly with your fingers. Using a cocktail stick (toothpick), make light indentations in the paste in vertical lines at evenly spaced intervals around the ball. Then create a hollow in the top.

2 Roll the brown sugarpaste into a short fat sausage and attach to the hollow with a dab of water.

3 Position the pumpkin on the top of the filled and piped push pop.

creepy option...
To transform your pumpkin into a jack-o'-lantern for Halloween, draw on a scary expression with a black edible ink pen.

Recipes mini cupcakes, frostings & fillings
Techniques making push pops

bump in the night

The kids will be banging your door down this Halloween to get their hands on these terrifying treats!

you will need...

makes 3

- ♡ 3 filled push pops of your choice piped high with a 1cm (½in) round piping tube (tip)
- ♡ 50g (1¾oz) white sugarpaste (rolled fondant)
- ♡ 9cm (3½in) circle cutter
- ♡ black edible ink pen

1 Roll out the white sugarpaste to 2mm (⅟₁₆in) thick. Using the circle cutter, cut out three circles.

2 Gently place each circle on a filled and piped push pop and use your fingers to arrange the hanging paste into ruffles and folds.

3 Using a black edible ink pen, draw a pair of large, hollow-looking eyes onto each ghost.

Recipes mini cupcakes, frostings & fillings
Techniques making push pops, rolling out paste, using cutters

down the rabbit hole

Take a magical tour down the rabbit hole with these entertaining Easter bunny-themed push pops.

you will need...

makes 1

- ♡ 1 chocolate push pop filled and piped with vanilla buttercream tinted green with paste food colour

- ♡ sugarpaste (rolled fondant): 50g (1¾oz) white and 5g (⅛oz) pink sugarpaste

1 For the bunny's bottom, roll 30g (generous 1oz) of the white sugarpaste into a ball. Flatten one side of the ball to make a semicircular shape.

2 For the feet, mould 15g (½oz) of the white sugarpaste into two small ovals. Form the pink sugarpaste into one larger pad and three smaller pads for each foot, then attach with a little water. Using a dab of water, attach each foot to the bunny's bottom.

3 For the fluffy tail, roll the remaining white sugarpaste into a ball and prick it all over with a cocktail stick (toothpick). Attach the tail to the bunny's bottom with a dab of water and leave to dry for 1 hour.

4 Position the bunny on top of the filled and piped push pop as if he were disappearing down into the frosting.

Recipes mini cupcakes, frostings & fillings
Techniques making push pops, colouring frostings

bunny ears

Why not give these adorable push pops rather than chocolate eggs for Easter – they'll be much more memorable.

you will need...

makes 3

- ♡ 3 vanilla push pops filled and piped with vanilla buttercream
- ♡ flower (petal/gum) paste: 20g (¾oz) each white and pink
- ♡ large and medium leaf cutter

1 Roll out the white and pink flower pastes very thinly. Using the large leaf cutter, cut out six leaves from the white paste, then the medium leaf cutter to cut out six leaves from the pink paste.

2 Using a dab of water, attach each pink leaf to the bottom centre of a white leaf to create three sets of ears. Leave to dry for several hours or overnight on a tray lined with cling film (plastic wrap).

3 Position each pair of bunny ears on the top of a filled and piped push pop.

Recipes mini cupcakes, frostings & fillings
Techniques making push pops, rolling out paste, using cutters

4ᵗʰ of July

This star-spangled design is a breeze to create and guaranteed to make the celebrations go with a pop.

you will need...

makes 3

- ♡ 3 filled and frosted push pops of your choice
- ♡ flower (petal/gum) paste: 30g (generous 1oz) red, 20g (¾oz) blue, 10g (½oz) white
- ♡ small amount of white royal icing
- ♡ disposable plastic piping (pastry) bag fitted with a no. 2 piping tube (tip)
- ♡ large, medium and small star cutters

1 Roll out each flower paste colour to 2mm (¹⁄₁₆in) thick. Using the large star cutter, cut three stars from the red petal paste, then use the medium star cutter to cut three stars from the blue paste and the small star cutter to cut three stars from the white paste. Leave the paste stars to dry for several hours or overnight.

2 Place the royal icing in the piping bag and pipe a dot onto each red star, then attach each blue star to a red star, slightly off centre. Repeat to attach each white star to a blue star. Leave to dry for 1 hour.

3 Position a star decoration on top of each filled and piped push pop.

Recipes mini cupcakes, frostings & fillings
Techniques making push pops, rolling out paste, using cutters

hey little pilgrim

What better way to round off your Thanksgiving fest than with these super-cute little pilgrim hats.

you will need...

makes 3

- ♡ **3 filled and flat-frosted push pops of your choice**
- ♡ **sugarpaste (rolled fondant): 50g (1¾oz) black, 10g (¼oz) yellow**
- ♡ **empty push pop container**

1 To make the hat brims, roll out the black sugarpaste to 2mm (¹⁄₁₆in) thick. Using the empty push pop container, cut out three circles. Place each one on a filled and flat-frosted push pop.

2 Divide the remaining black sugarpaste into three pieces and mould each into a crown for the hat brims. Using a dab of water, attach the crowns to the brims.

3 Roll out the yellow sugarpaste very thinly. Using a very sharp craft knife, cut out three buckle shapes. Attach each buckle to a hat with a dab of water.

Recipes mini cupcakes, frostings & fillings
Techniques making push pops, rolling out paste, cutting paste by hand

lovehearts

Sweets for your sweet. Woo and wow that special someone on Valentine's Day with these heartfelt push pops.

you will need...

makes 1

- ♡ 1 filled and piped push pop of your choice
- ♡ 20g (1¾oz) pink flower (petal/gum) paste
- ♡ small amount of royal icing tinted brown with paste food colour
- ♡ disposable plastic piping (pastry) bag fitted with a no. 2 piping tube (tip)
- ♡ 5cm (2in) heart cutter

1 Roll out the pink flower paste very thinly. Using the heart cutter, cut out a heart. Leave to dry for a several hours or overnight.

2 Place the brown-tinted royal icing in the piping bag and pipe the initials of yourself and your loved one on the heart. Leave the heart to dry for 1 hour.

3 Position the heart on top of the filled and piped push pop.

Recipes mini cupcakes, frostings & fillings

Techniques making push pops, rolling out paste, using cutters, colouring frostings, piping details

sealed with a kiss

Go on and give your loved one a big soppy kiss for Valentine's in the form of these lip-smacking push pops.

you will need...

makes 1

- ♡ 1 filled and piped push pop of your choice
- ♡ 50g (1¾oz) red sugarpaste (rolled fondant)
- ♡ *red edible glitter
- ♡ cornflour (cornstarch), for dusting
- ♡ boiled water left to cool
- ♡ silicone lips mould
- ♡ baking (parchment) paper

* If product not certified edible, please remove before eating

1 Using a small paintbrush, brush the inside of the lips mould with cornflour to prevent the sugarpaste from sticking to the design. Take the red sugarpaste and press it firmly into the mould.

2 Release the lips by turning the mould upside down. Dust off any cornflour left on the lips with the paintbrush.

3 Place the lips on a square of baking (parchment) paper. Again using the paintbrush, lightly paint the lips with cooled boiled water. Sprinkle red edible glitter over the lips, making sure they are completely covered.

4 Position the sparkly lips on top of your filled and piped push pop.

saving grace...
Pour the excess glitter back into its container for next time.

Recipes mini cupcakes, frostings & fillings
Techniques making push pops, using moulds, glitter & dust

New Year's rockin' eve

Count down to the New Year in style with this sensational centrepiece of numbered push pops arranged to create a clock face.

you will need...

makes 12

- ♡ 12 filled and flat-frosted push pops of your choice
- ♡ 300g (10½oz) white sugarpaste (rolled fondant)
- ♡ 50g (1¾oz) royal icing tinted black with paste food colour
- ♡ empty push pop container
- ♡ disposable plastic piping (pastry) bag fitted with a no. 2 piping tube (tip)
- ♡ 12 Champagne flutes
- ♡ black card

1 Roll out the sugarpaste to around 3mm (⅛in) thick. Using the open end of an empty push pop container, cut out 12 circles.

2 Place the black-tinted royal icing in the piping bag and pipe a number from 1 to 12 on each circle. Leave to dry overnight.

3 Place a piped circle on top of each filled and flat-frosted push pop. Place each push pop in a Champagne flute and arrange in a circle with the numbers in sequence to resemble a clock.

4 Cut out two clock hands, one shorter and one longer, from black card and place the shorter hand pointing to 12 o'clock and the longer hand pointing to 10 o'clock.

Recipes mini cupcakes, frostings & fillings

Techniques making push pops, rolling out paste, colouring frostings, piping details

for fun

cutie creepy crawlies

These bugs are definitely the fun and friendly kind that anyone would welcome into their garden – in fact, they're good enough to eat!

you will need...

makes 3

- ♡ 3 push pops of your choice filled and piped high with a 1cm (½in) round piping tube (tip)
- ♡ sugarpaste (rolled fondant): 50g (1¾oz) each yellow and red, 75g (2¾oz) black, 6g (generous ⅛oz) white
- ♡ 4 flaked (slivered) almonds
- ♡ *white edible lustre dust
- ♡ circle cutters: 7cm (2¾in), 1cm (⅜in)
- ♡ black edible ink pen

* If product not certified edible, please remove before eating

1 Roll out the yellow, red and black sugarpastes to 2mm (¹⁄₁₆in) thick and use a cutter to cut a 7cm (2¾in) circle from each. Gently place each circle on a filled and piped push pop and smooth it down to create a mound.

2 For the bee Roll out the remaining black sugarpaste and cut out a 7cm (2¾in) circle. Cut into stripes 1cm (⅜in) wide, cutting one with a curved edge for the face. Attach to the yellow push pop with a dab of water. For eyes, roll 2g (¹⁄₁₆oz) of the white sugarpaste into two balls and stick in place with a dab of water. Using a black edible ink pen, add dots for pupils. Push the flaked almonds into the centre of the body for wings.

3 For the ladybug Roll out the remaining black sugarpaste and cut out a 7cm (2¾in) circle. Cut a strip from the curved edge for the face, then cut six 1cm (⅜in) circles with a cutter from the remaining paste. Using a dab of water, attach the face and spots to the red push pop. Make the eyes and add pupils as for the bee.

4 For the beetle Using the side of a cocktail stick (toothpick), make shallow indentations in the black push pop to create the wing casing. Brush the paste with white edible lustre dust to create a shiny outer shell effect. Make the eyes and add pupils as for the bee.

Recipes mini cupcakes, frostings & fillings

Techniques making push pops, rolling out paste, using cutters, cutting paste by hand, glitter & dust

flutterby

Topped with pretty little butterflies, these push pops will flutter their way right into your heart.

you will need...

makes 3

- ♡ 3 vanilla push pops filled and piped with vanilla buttercream tinted green with paste food colour
- ♡ flower (petal/gum) paste: 30g (generous 1oz) each pink and blue
- ♡ veined butterfly plunger cutter
- ♡ folded piece of card

1 Roll out the pink and blue flower paste colours very thinly and use the plunger cutter to cut out two butterflies from each colour, remembering to push down on the plunger to create the patterned wings. Leave the butterflies to dry overnight in a folded piece of card.

2 Position one pink and one blue butterfly on top of each filled and piped push pop.

after effects...
Once dry, paint a fine line of gold edible lustre dust down each butterfly body and/or sprinkle the wings with white edible glitter. If the products used are not certified edible, please remove the butterflies before eating the cakes.

Recipes mini cupcakes, frostings & fillings
Techniques making push pops, rolling out paste, using cutters, colouring frostings, glitter & dust

cats & dogs

Please all those pet lovers with these lovable animal-adorned push pops – great for any occasion.

you will need...

makes 2

- ♡ 2 push pops of your choice filled and piped with a 1cm (½in) round piping tube (tip)

- ♡ sugarpaste (rolled fondant): 50g (1¾oz) each brown and black, 20g (¾oz) white, 15g (½oz) pink

- ♡ circle cutters: 7cm (2¾in), 3cm (1¼in)

- ♡ black edible ink pen

1 Roll out the brown and black sugarpastes to 2mm (¹⁄₁₆in) thick and use a cutter to cut out a 7cm (2¾in) circle from each. Gently place each circle on a filled and piped push pop and smooth it down to create a mound.

2 For the dog From the brown paste, cut an upside-down heart shape 3cm (1¼in) high for a muzzle and two teardrops 4cm (1½in) high for ears. Using a dab of cold water, attach in place to the brown push pop.

3 For eyes, roll 5g (⅛oz) of the white sugarpaste into two balls and stick in place with water, then attach two small flattened black paste balls for pupils and a larger black ball for a nose. For a tongue, mould 5g (⅛oz) of the pink sugarpaste into a small fat teardrop and attach just under the mouth. Use a cocktail stick (toothpick) to add the details to the muzzle.

4 For the cat Cut two fat teardrops 1cm (⅜in) high from black paste for ears and attach to the top of the black push pop. Add two small flattened pink paste balls for inner ears. Roll out the white paste to 2mm (¹⁄₁₆in) thick, cut out a 3cm (1¼in) circle and attach in place.

5 Attach two small white paste balls for eyes and add tiny flattened black paste balls for pupils. Indent the cheeks with a cocktail stick. Add a small pink paste ball for a nose. Draw on a mouth with the edible pen.

Recipes mini cupcakes, frostings & fillings

Techniques making push pops, rolling out paste, using cutters, cutting paste by hand

football fanatic

Every day can be Superbowl Sunday with these delicious push pops topped with convincing-looking footballs.

you will need...

makes 1

- ♡ 1 Mint Chocolate Chip push pop (see Fabulous Flavours)
- ♡ 20g (¾oz) brown sugarpaste (rolled fondant)
- ♡ small amount of white royal icing
- ♡ disposable plastic piping (pastry) bag fitted with a no. 2 piping tube (tip)

1 For the football, mould the brown sugarpaste into an oval, bringing the ends to a rounded point.

2 Place the royal icing in the piping bag and pipe the laces onto the football. Leave to dry for 1 hour.

3 Position the ball on top of the filled and piped push pop.

Recipes mini cupcakes, frostings & fillings
Techniques making push pops, colouring frostings, piping details

precious teddy

In a twist on the well-known song about teddies, today's the day the teddy bear *is* the picnic!

you will need...

makes 1

- ♡ 1 filled and flat-frosted chocolate push pop
- ♡ sugarpaste (rolled fondant): 100g (3½oz) brown, 5g (⅛oz) black
- ♡ 5cm (2in) length of dried spaghetti
- ♡ black edible ink pen

1 For the body, mould 55g (2oz) of the brown sugarpaste into a barrel shape with a flat base about the same diameter as the push pop container. Place the base on the filled and flat-frosted push pop.

2 For the head, roll 20g (¾oz) of the brown paste into a ball. Mould two ears from another 5g (⅛oz). Attach to the top of the head with a dab of water. Add the indentations with a cocktail stick (toothpick).

3 Insert the spaghetti (remove before eating) into the centre of the body, leaving 2.5cm (1in) protruding, then push the head onto the end.

4 For the arms, roll the remaining brown paste into two curved and tapered sausages 3cm (1¼in) long. Flatten one end of each sausage and attach to either side of the body. Use the cocktail stick to make indentations for paws and a line of stitch holes down the tummy.

5 For the nose, attach a flattened ball of the black sugarpaste with a dab of water. Draw on the eyes and mouth with the black edible pen.

Recipes mini cupcakes, frostings & fillings
Techniques making push pops

country garden

Capture the wonder of a country garden in full bloom with these push pop beauties embellished with vibrant yellow sunflowers and vivid blue petunias.

you will need...

makes 4

- ♡ push pops: 2 of your choice plus 2 Pocketful of Posies (see Popping Occasions), all filled and piped with buttercream tinted green with paste food colour

- ♡ 50g (1¾oz) yellow flower (petal/gum) paste

- ♡ 10g (¼oz) brown sugarpaste (rolled fondant)

- ♡ medium daisy plunger cutter

- ♡ paint palette

* If product not certified edible, please remove before eating

1 Roll out the yellow flower paste very thinly. Using the plunger cutter, cut out two sunflowers. Leave to dry in a separate wells of a paint palette for several hours or overnight.

2 Divide the brown sugarpaste in half and roll each piece of paste into a ball. Flatten each ball into a disc, then indent small holes with a cocktail stick (toothpick). Using a dab of water, attach a disc to the centre of each sunflower.

3 Attach one sunflower to the top of each undecorated filled and piped push pop. Intersperse with the petunia-decorated push pops to create your country garden display.

Recipes mini cupcakes, frostings & fillings
Techniques making push pops, colouring frostings, rolling out paste, using cutters

enchanted forest

Push pops decorated with fairy toadstools introduced into a grouping of flower and butterfly designs creates a magical, fantastical scene.

you will need...

makes 8

- ♡ push pops: 2 of your choice piped with buttercream tinted with green paste food colour, plus 2 of each flower design from Country Garden and 2 Flutterby

- ♡ sugarpaste (rolled fondant): 50g (1¾oz) each white and red

- ♡ plastic drinking straw

1 For the toadstool bases, mould 30g (generous 1oz) of the white sugarpaste into four fat cones.

2 For the toadstool spots, roll out the remaining white sugarpaste to 2mm (¹⁄₁₆in) thick. Using the end of a plastic drinking straw, cut out about 24 small circles.

3 For the tops of the toadstools, mould the red sugarpaste into four larger fat cones and round off one end of each into a dome shape.

4 Using dabs of water, attach each toadstool top to a base, then attach about six of the white spots, evenly spaced, on each toadstool top.

5 Position two toadstools on top of each undecorated filled and piped push pop. Then arrange these among the Country Garden and Flutterby push pops.

Recipes mini cupcakes, frostings & fillings
Techniques making push pops, colouring frostings, rolling out paste

alien attack!

You have been warned – prepare yourself for a close encounter of the sweet kind! These push pops are as fun to make as they are to eat.

you will need...

makes 1

- ♡ 1 push pop of your choice filled and piped with a 1cm (½in) round piping tube (tip)
- ♡ sugarpaste (rolled fondant): 50g (1¾oz) green, 10g (¼oz) white
- ♡ 1 piece of dried spaghetti, broken into 4cm (1½in) lengths
- ♡ 7cm (2¾in) circle cutter
- ♡ black edible ink pen

1 Roll out the green sugarpaste to around 2mm (¹⁄₁₆in) thick. Using the cutter, cut out a circle. Gently place the circle on the filled and piped push pop and smooth it down to create a mound.

2 Using a black edible ink pen, draw a large dot on the centre front of the green mound for a mouth.

3 Divide the white sugarpaste into three pieces, then roll each into a ball. Use the black edible pen to draw a dot in the centre of each ball.

4 Insert a length of spaghetti into the bottom of each ball, then gently insert the spaghetti stems into the green mound in a row. Remove the spaghetti stems before eating.

Recipes mini cupcakes, frostings & fillings
Techniques making push pops, rolling out paste, using cutters

splish splash

These push pops encapsulate the delights of bathtub playtime with toy duck friends, lovingly recreated here in sugarpaste.

you will need...

makes 1

- ♡ 1 vanilla push pop filled and piped with vanilla buttercream tinted with blue paste food colour
- ♡ sugarpaste (rolled fondant): 35g (1¼oz) yellow, 5g (⅛oz) orange
- ♡ black edible ink pen
- ♡ white sprinkles (nonpareils)

1 For the duck's body, mould 20g (¾oz) of the yellow sugarpaste into a fat teardrop shape. For the head, roll another 10g (¼oz) of the paste into a ball.

2 For the wings, divide the remaining yellow sugarpaste in half and shape each into a small, flat teardrop. Using a dab of water, attach the head and wings to the body.

3 For the beak, mould the orange sugarpaste into a small cone shape and attach to the head with a small dab of water.

4 For the eyes, use a black edible ink pen to add a dot either side of the head.

5 Place the duck on top of the filled and piped push pop and scatter a few white sprinkles around your duck to resemble bubbles.

Recipes mini cupcakes, frostings & fillings
Techniques making push pops, colouring frostings

jolly roger

You'll be the scourge of the seven seas with these piratical Jolly Roger-themed push pops.

you will need...

makes 1

- ♡ 1 filled and piped push pop of your choice
- ♡ 50g (1¾oz) white sugarpaste (rolled fondant)
- ♡ *black edible glitter
- ♡ cornflour (cornstarch), for dusting
- ♡ boiled water left to cool
- ♡ silicone skull and crossbones mould

*If product not certified edible, please remove before eating

1 Using a small paintbrush, brush the inside of the skull and crossbones mould with cornflour to prevent the sugarpaste from sticking to the design. Take the white sugarpaste and press it firmly into the mould.

2 Release the skull and crossbones by turning the mould upside down. Dust off any cornflour left on the moulded shape with the paintbrush.

3 Again using the paintbrush, paint the inside of the eye sockets with the cooled boiled water. Dry off your paintbrush and then use to paint black edible glitter into the hollows of the eyes. Leave the skull and crossbones to dry for a few hours or overnight.

4 Position the skull and crossbones on top of your filled and piped push pop.

Recipes mini cupcakes, frostings & fillings
Techniques making push pops, using moulds, glitter & dust

ombre push pops

These ombre-themed push pops are stunning for a wedding or birthday celebration - a bit harder to make than a regular push pop, but well worth the effort.

you will need...

makes 6

- ♡ 1 batch vanilla mini cupcakes batter
- ♡ 1 batch vanilla buttercream
- ♡ pink paste food colour
- ♡ 3 x 23cm (9in) sandwich (round shallow) cake tins (pans) lined with baking (parchment) paper
- ♡ disposable plastic piping (pastry) bag fitted with a no. 1M (WIL) piping tube (tip)

1 Preheat your oven to 160°C/fan 140°C/325°F/Gas Mark 3. Divide the cupcake batter equally between three bowls. Using a cocktail stick (toothpick), add pink paste food colour to the bowls so that the batter in each is a darker pink than the one before.

2 Pour each batch of batter into a prepared tin and bake in the oven for 20 minutes. Allow to cool in the tins for 5 minutes before turning out to finish cooling on a wire rack.

3 Once cool, level your cakes by cutting off the domed tops. Using one of your push pop containers, cut six coins of cake from each cake.

5 Assemble each of your push pops, starting with the darkest pink cake layer. Then place the buttercream in the piping bag and pipe a tiny amount of frosting on top.

6 Repeat Step 5 with the lighter pink cake layer, then add the palest pink layer. Finish off each push pop by piping a swirl of frosting on top.

Recipes mini cupcakes, frostings & fillings
Techniques making push pops, colouring cake batters

suppliers

UK

Cakes, Cookies & Crafts
Unit 2, Francis Business Park,
White Lund Industrial Estate,
Morecamble,
Lancashire, LA3 3PT
Tel: 01524 389684
www.cakescookiesandcraftsshop.co.uk

Design-a-Cake
30–31 Phoenix Road,
Crowther Industrial Estate,
Washington,
Tyne and Wear, NE38 OAD
Tel: 0191 4177377
www.design-a-cake.co.uk

Hobbycraft
Stores nationwide
Tel: 0845 051 6599
www.hobbycraft.co.uk

Lakeland
Stores nationwide
Tel: 015394 88100
www.lakeland.co.uk

Stitch Craft Create
Brunel House, Forde Close,
Newton Abbot, TQ12 4PU
Tel: 0844 880 5852
www.stitchcraftcreate.co.uk

USA

Global Sugar Art
625 Route 3, Unit 3,
Plattsburgh, NY 12901
Tel: + 1 800 420 6088
www.globalsugarart.com

US Cake Supply
TCP Global,
6695 Rasha Street,
San Diego, CA 92121-2241
Tel: + 1 858 909 2110
www.uscakesupply.com

Wilton Industries
2240 West 75th Street,
Woodridge, IL 60517
Tel: + 1 800 794 5866
www.wilton.com

Abbreviation
WIL = Wilton

about the author

Katie Deacon is the co-owner of the adorable cupcake boutique Pet Lamb Patisserie, along with her best friend Kay, for which she designs and creates beautiful and delicious cupcakes to be enjoyed by all.

Katie is also the writer of the popular online baking blog Katiecakes, and has appeared in countless magazines and TV shows.

Ever passionate about all things cake, Katie can't wait to see what her frosting-filled future holds!

acknowledgments

I'd like to thank the whole team over at David & Charles for their constant support and encouragement throughout the whole process. Special thanks go out to James and Jo for their everlasting patience and attention to detail.

A special shout out to my partner in crime and the other half of Pet Lamb Patisserie, Kay. Thank you for keeping me sane and always being the voice of reason. To my family, thank you for always gratefully eating everything I've ever brought you. Whether burned, undercooked or just plain wrong, you never let on.

Finally, I'd like to thank my wonderful fiancée amd patient photographer, Kris. Without your support and encouragement I would never have come so far. If not for you and the cats, I'd be half the woman I am today.

index

A DAVID & CHARLES BOOK
© F&W Media International, LTD 2013

David & Charles is an imprint of F&W Media
International, Ltd
Brunel House, Forde Close, Newton Abbot,
TQ12 4PU, UK

F&W Media International, Ltd is a subsidiary
of F+W Media, Inc
10151 Carver Road, Suite #200, Blue Ash,
OH 45242, USA

First published in the UK and USA in 2013

Text and designs copyright © Katie Deacon 2013
Layout and photography © F&W Media
International, LTD 2013

Katie Deacon has asserted her right to
be identified as author of this work in
accordance with the Copyright, Designs
and Patents Act, 1988.

A catalogue record for this book is available
from the British Library.

ISBN-13: 978-1-4463-0306-1 hardback
ISBN-10: 1-4463-0306-3 hardback

Printed in China by RR Donnelley
for F&W Media International, LTD
Brunel House, Forde Close, Newton Abbot,
TQ12 4PU, UK

10 9 8 7 6 5 4 3 2 1

Publisher Alison Myer
Junior Acquisitions Editor James Brooks
Assistant Editor Grace Harvey
Project Editor Jo Richardson
Art Editor Sarah Underhill
Designers Lucy Parissi and Jenny Stanley
Senior Production Controller Kelly Smith
Photographer Kris Stewart

F+W Media publishes high-quality books on a
wide range of subjects. For more great book
ideas visit: **www.stitchcraftcreate.co.uk**

loved this book?

For more inspiration, ideas and free downloadable projects visit **www.stitchcraftcreate.co.uk**

Bake Me I'm Yours...
Cupcake Fun
Carolyn White
ISBN-13: 978-1-4463-0242-2

Learn how to design, bake and decorate fun sugar characters with this collection of over 30 cupcake designs. From princesses and pirates to firemen, policemen and nurses, each project is quick and easy to make – perfect presents for children's parties or school events!

Bake Me I'm Yours...
Whoopie Pies
Jill Collins & Natalie Saville
ISBN-13: 978-1-4463-0068-8

Discover over 70 designs that will make you shout 'whoopie!' These gorgeous (and tasty!) baked treats are organized into fun themed collections of coordinating whoopies for any celebration.

Bake Me I'm Yours...
Cake Pops
Carolyn White
ISBN-13: 978-1-4463-0137-1

A delicious collection of fun cake pop treats for every occasion, with over 40 colourful projects, from cute animals and romantic wedding rings, to creepy Halloween creatures and festive Christmas characters!

Bake Me I'm Yours...
Sweet Bitesize Bakes
Sarah Trivuncic
ISBN-13: 978-1-4463-0183-8

Bake miniature versions of your best-loved desserts, confections and sweet treats with these easy-to-follow recipes, including tasty fillings and toppings, from buttercream and chocolate ganache to marshmallow fluff, lemon curd and crème pâtissière.